THIS BOOK BELONGS TO:

Copyright © 2020 Soulpress

Concept by Jamie Flynn Ruben. No part of this book may be reproduced or used in any manner without written permission of the copyright owner except for the use of quotations in a book review.

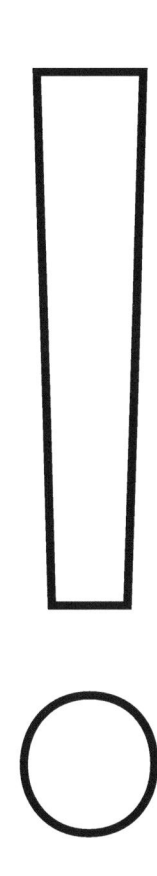

Some pens and markers stain through paper.
To avoid bleed-through problems and frustration,
please use colored pencils or place a sheet of paper
underneath the page you are currently coloring.

CREME BRULEE LATTE

Yield: 1

INGREDIENTS:

6 oz (180 ml) brewed coffee
1 oz (30 ml) hot milk
1 tsp of vanilla extract or syrup
1 tbsp caramel syrup
Brown sugar (to taste)
Whipped cream
Garnish with toffee bits
and caramel sauce

HOW TO MAKE:

Pour some freshly brewed coffee in a mug. Add hot milk, brown sugar, and vanilla extract, and stir well until the sugar is dissolved. Top off with whipped cream, caramel sauce, and toffee bits.

CINNAMON CAPPUCCINO

Yield: 1

INGREDIENTS:

2 shots (60 ml) espresso
2 oz (60 ml) frothed milk
1-2 tsp cinnamon syrup
Garnish: a dash of cinnamon

HOW TO MAKE:

Pour the espresso shots into a coffee cup. Froth the milk with a frothing wand together with the cinnamon syrup, and slowly pour the mixture into the cup, on top of the espresso shots. Finally, complete your cappuccino with a dash of cinnamon or unsweetened cocoa powder.

COFFEE CHIA PUDDING

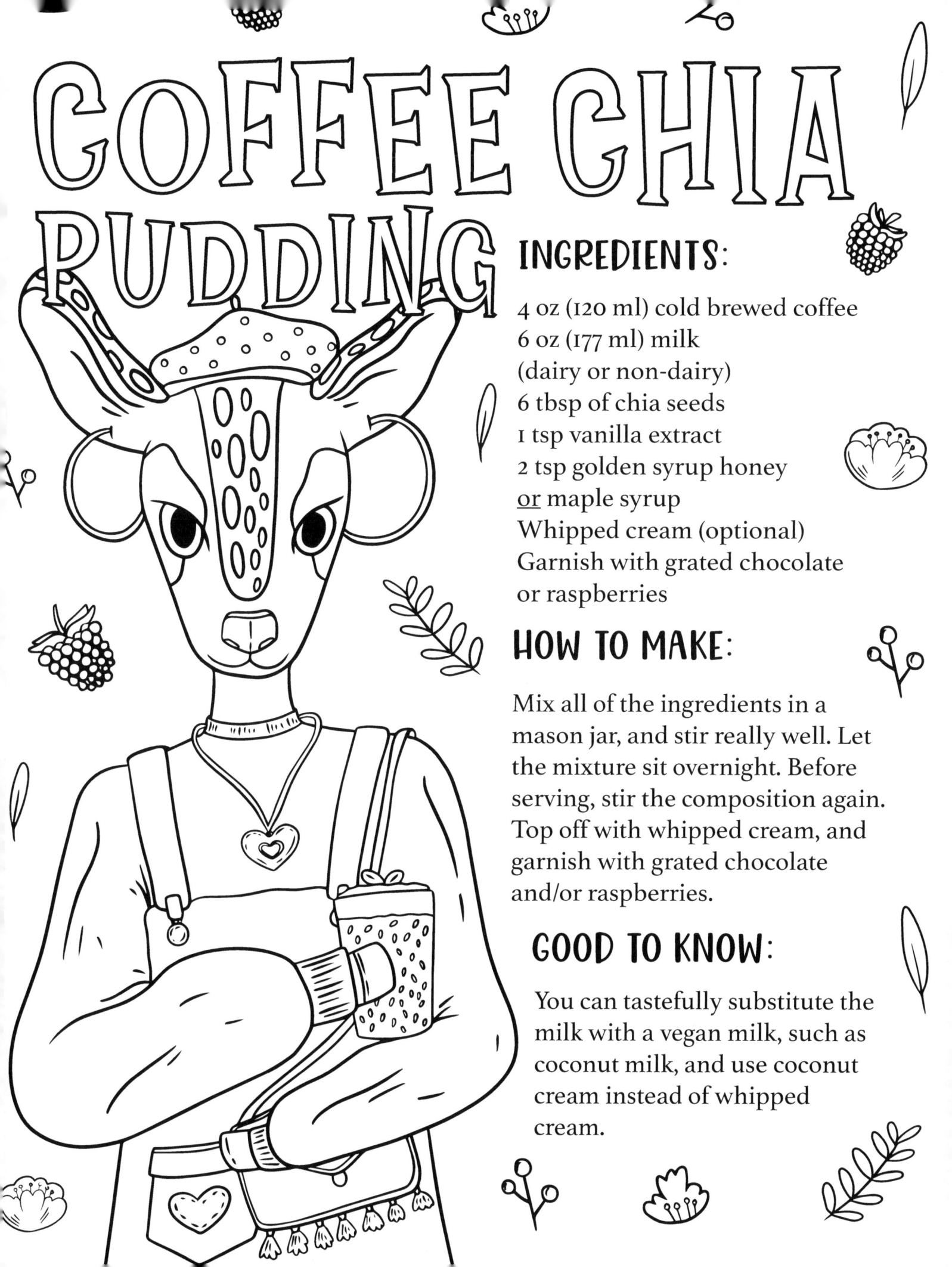

INGREDIENTS:

4 oz (120 ml) cold brewed coffee
6 oz (177 ml) milk
(dairy or non-dairy)
6 tbsp of chia seeds
1 tsp vanilla extract
2 tsp golden syrup honey
<u>or</u> maple syrup
Whipped cream (optional)
Garnish with grated chocolate
or raspberries

HOW TO MAKE:

Mix all of the ingredients in a mason jar, and stir really well. Let the mixture sit overnight. Before serving, stir the composition again. Top off with whipped cream, and garnish with grated chocolate and/or raspberries.

GOOD TO KNOW:

You can tastefully substitute the milk with a vegan milk, such as coconut milk, and use coconut cream instead of whipped cream.

PUMPKIN SPICE LATTE

INGREDIENTS: Yield: 1

1-2 shots (30-60 ml) of espresso
or 2 oz (60 ml) brewed coffee
6 oz (177 ml) milk or almond milk
1 tbsp maple syrup (to taste)
1 tbsp pumpkin puree
2 tsp vanilla extract
1/2 tsp pumpkin pie spice
Whipped cream

HOW TO MAKE:

Add the milk, pumpkin puree, vanilla extract, pumpkin pie spice, and maple syrup in a pan and heat until the mixture is hot - do not bring it to a boil! Whisk the mixture vigorously until you get a foamy texture. Pour espresso shots or freshly brewed coffee into a mug, and add in your pumpkin mixture. Top off with whipped cream (optional), and sprinkle with some pumpkin pie spice.

To create your own pumpkin pie spice blend, simply combine 1/2 tsp ground cinnamon, 1/4 tsp ground ginger, 1/8 tsp ground nutmeg, and 1/8 tsp ground cloves.

NUTELLA FRAPPE

Yield: 1

INGREDIENTS:

1-2 shots (30-60 ml) espresso
6 oz (175 ml) milk or coconut milk
1-2 tbsp of Nutella
(or any chocolate spread)
1 cup ice cubes
Whipped cream
Garnish: 2 chocolate sticks

HOW TO MAKE:

Mix Nutella with 1-2 shots of espresso. Stir until melted. In a blender, add the coffee and Nutella mixture with your choice of milk and ice. Blend until smooth. Pour it into a large milkshake glass and top off with whipped cream and two chocolate sticks.

GINGERBREAD LATTE

INGREDIENTS:

Yield: 1

1.5 oz (45 ml) brewed coffee
or 1 oz (30 ml) espresso
4 oz (120 ml) steamed milk
4 oz (120 ml) water
1 tsp ground ginger
1/2 tsp ground cinnamon
1/2 cup brown sugar
1 tsp vanilla extract
1/4 tsp nutmeg
Whipped cream

HOW TO MAKE:

Make the gingerbread syrup by mixing water, ground ginger, brown sugar, cinnamon, and vanilla extract in a pan. Over low heat, stir the mixture until all ingredients are well mixed and dissolved. Add 2 tbsp of gingerbread syrup (or more), the espresso shot (or brewed coffee) and steamed milk to a glass, and stir well. Top off with whipped cream, and sprinkle some nutmeg on top.

CARAMEL LATTE

INGREDIENTS:

Yield: 1

1 -1.5 oz (30-45 ml) brewed coffee
6 oz (180 ml) milk (or coconut milk)
1-2 tbsp caramel syrup
1 tsp sugar (optional, to taste)
Whipped cream (optional)
Garnish with caramel sauce

HOW TO MAKE:

Combine your choice of milk, caramel syrup, and sugar in a small pan and heat the mixture on low until both the caramel syrup and sugar are well mixed and dissolved. Whisk vigorously until foamy. Pour 1-2 shots of espresso or freshly brewed coffee into your favorite mug. Add the caramel mixture, and stir gently. Top off with whipped cream if desired, and garnish with caramel sauce

COCONUT COFFEE FRAPPE

INGREDIENTS:

Yield: 1

6 oz (175 ml) chilled coffee
2 oz (60 ml) coconut milk
1 cups ice
2 tbsp heavy cream
Sugar (to taste)
1 tsp vanilla extract
Whipped cream
Garnish: chocolate sauce and biscuits

HOW TO MAKE:

Add ice, coffee, coconut milk, heavy cream, sugar, and vanilla extract in a blender. Blend for 2-3 minutes until the ice has broken up. Pour into a large glass, top off with whipped cream, and garnish with some chocolate sauce.

ESPRESSO MARTINI

Yield: 1

INGREDIENTS:

1 shot (30 ml) vanilla vodka
1 shot (30 ml) of espresso
1 shot (30 ml) of coffee liqueur
Ice cubes
Garnish: 3 whole coffee beans and a slice of orange

HOW TO MAKE:

Add all of the ingredients in a shaker filled with ice. Shake well until chilled. Fine strain into a cocktail glass, and garnish with an orange wedge and three coffee beans.

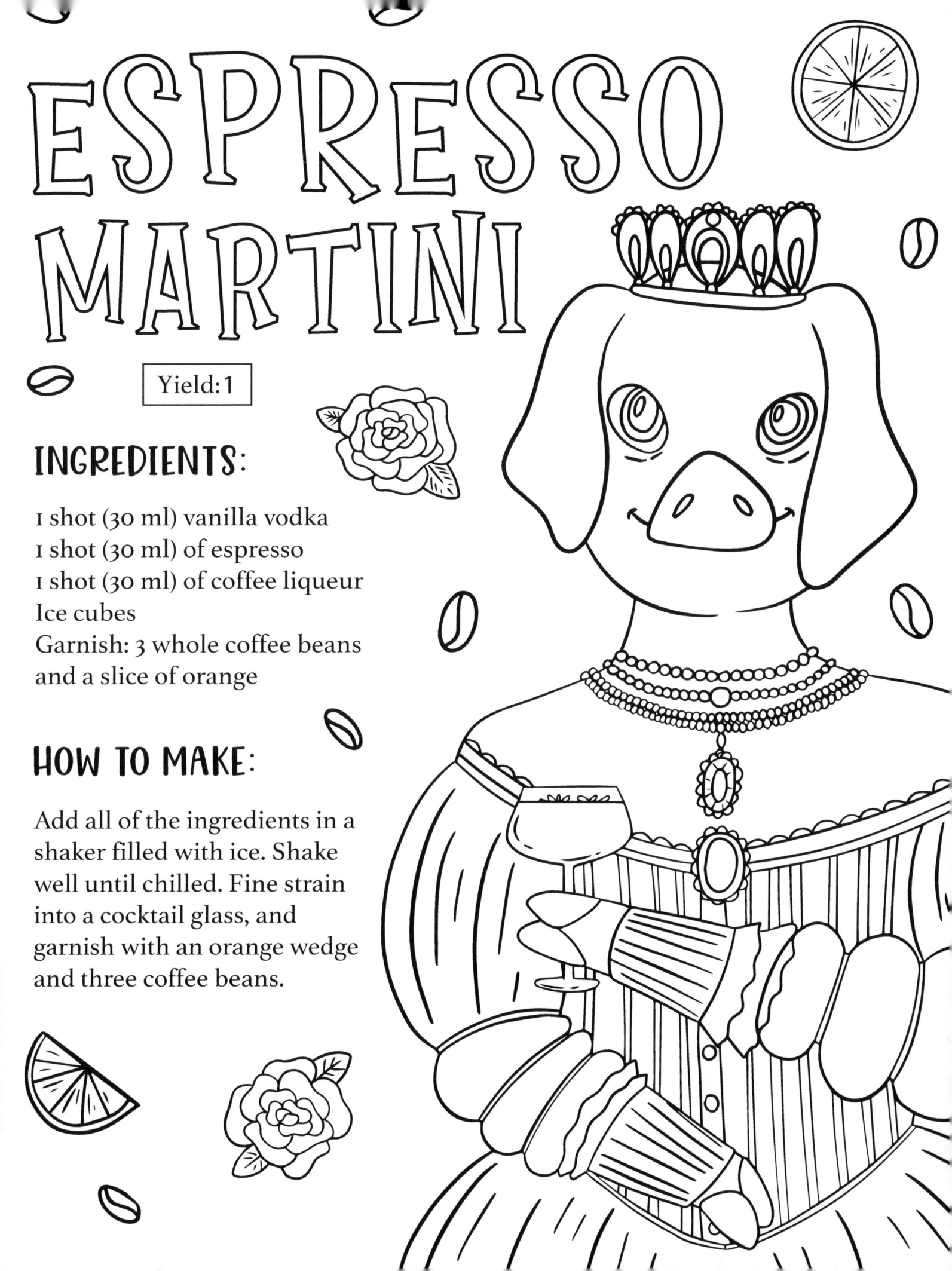

COFFEE CARAMEL MILKSHAKE

Yield: 1

HOW TO MAKE:

1-2 shots (30-60 ml) espresso
4 oz (120 ml) milk (dairy or non-dairy)
2 scoops vanilla ice cream
1 tbsp caramel syrup
Whipped cream
Garnish with caramel sauce

INGREDIENTS:

Blend together coffee, your choice of milk, ice cream scoops, and caramel syrup. Top off with whipped cream, and garnish with caramel sauce. Tasty, huh?

COFFEE MASCARPONE GRANOLA PARFAIT

INGREDIENTS:

Yield: 1

2 oz (55 g) mascarpone (at room temp)
1 heaped tbsp of sugar
0.3 oz (10 ml) espresso
2.9 oz (85 ml) cold whipping cream
1.3 oz (35 g) dark or milk chocolate
Granola cereals
Chocolate flakes for garnish

HOW TO MAKE:

Make the mascarpone and espresso cream by mixing together 1.6 oz cream, mascarpone cheese, espresso, and sugar. Whisk vigorously until you get a thick cream. Put the mixture in the refrigerator. In a pan, add the cream and your choice of chocolate. Then, heat and whisk until you get a uniform texture. Cool the chocolate cream at room temperature for 1 hour. In a tall glass, add a layer of chocolate cream, then a layer of granola cereals, and, finally, a layer of mascarpone and espresso cream. Repeat the entire layering process. Garnish with chocolate flakes.

VIENNESE COFFEE

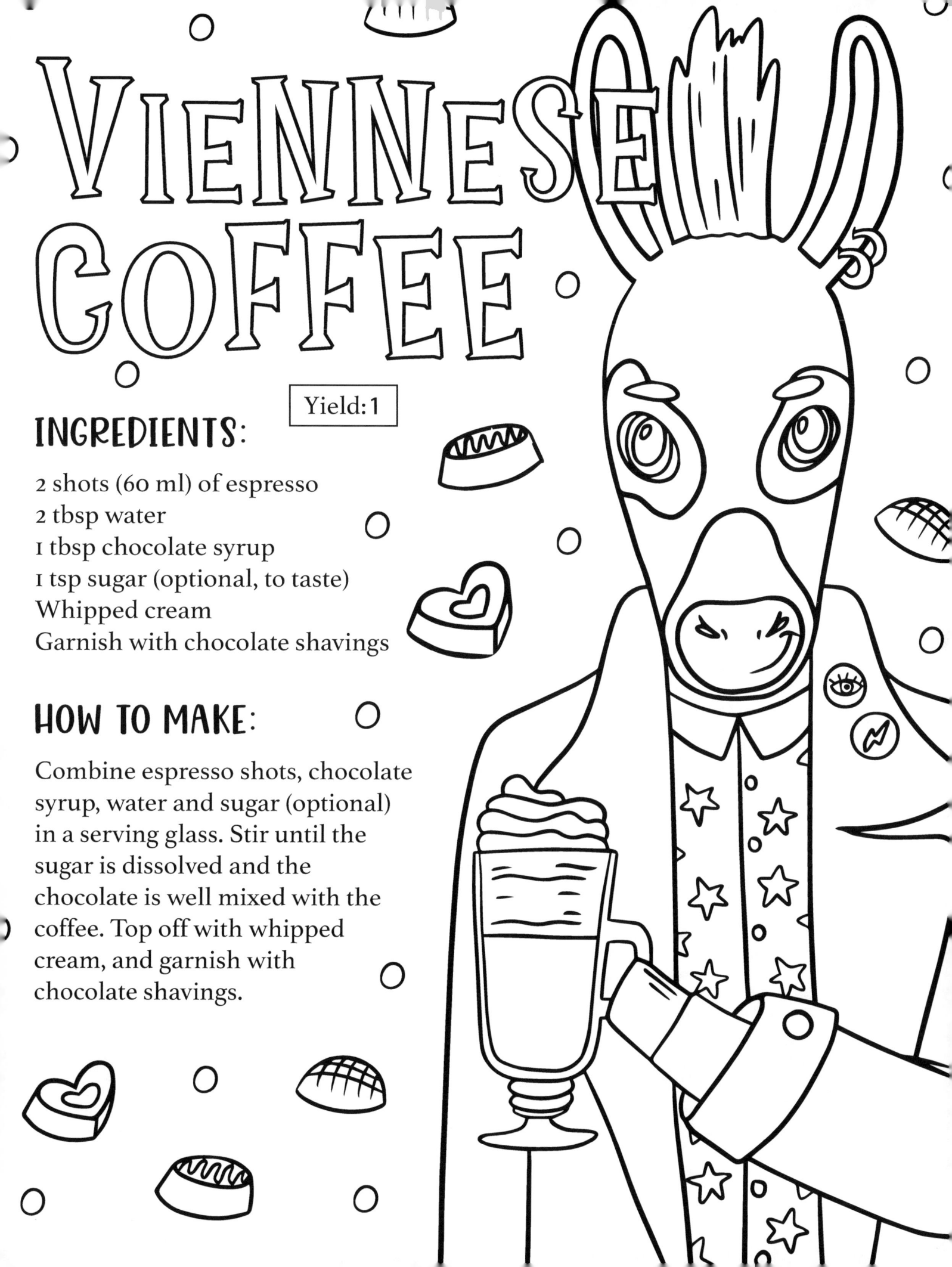

Yield: 1

INGREDIENTS:

2 shots (60 ml) of espresso
2 tbsp water
1 tbsp chocolate syrup
1 tsp sugar (optional, to taste)
Whipped cream
Garnish with chocolate shavings

HOW TO MAKE:

Combine espresso shots, chocolate syrup, water and sugar (optional) in a serving glass. Stir until the sugar is dissolved and the chocolate is well mixed with the coffee. Top off with whipped cream, and garnish with chocolate shavings.

COFFEE YOGURT POPS

Yield: 6

INGREDIENTS:

6 oz (180 ml) iced coffee
10 oz vanilla greek yogurt
1 tsp vanilla syrup or extract
6 popsicle molds

HOW TO MAKE:

Add coffee, vanilla greek yogurt, and vanilla syrup (or extract) in a bowl, and whisk until combined. Pour the mixture into popsicle molds, and let it chill in the freezer for a few hours.

COCONUT COLD BREW COFFEE

Yield: 1

INGREDIENTS:

4 oz (120 ml) cold brewed coffee
2.7 oz (80 ml) coconut milk
4 oz (120 ml) coconut water
Ice cubes (optional)

HOW TO MAKE:

To make this super easy coffee recipe, simply begin by adding some ice cubes (optional) into a mug or glass. Pour in cold brew coffee, coconut water, and coconut milk. Stir well, and enjoy.

CINNAMON VANILLA ICE COFFEE

INGREDIENTS:

Yield: 1

1.5 oz (45 ml) brewed coffee
or 1 shot (30 ml) espresso
5 oz (150 ml) milk (dairy or non-dairy)
1-2 tbsp vanilla syrup (to taste)
Ice cubes
Pinch of cinnamon
1 cinnamon stick for garnish

HOW TO MAKE:

In a glass half filled with ice, add coffee, vanilla syrup, and your choice of milk. Stir well. Garnish with a pinch of cinnamon and a cinnamon stick.

IRISH COFFEE

Yield: 1

INGREDIENTS:

1.5 oz (45 ml) Irish whiskey
6 oz (178 ml) strong brewed coffee
1 tsp brown sugar
Whipped cream
Chocolate shavings

HOW TO MAKE:

Take an Irish coffee mug (or your favorite mug) and add Irish whiskey, hot strong coffee and sugar (optional). Stir well. Add whipped cream on top. Garnish with chocolate shavings. Enjoy!

COFFEE ICE CREAM

Yield: 4

INGREDIENTS:

2-3 tbsp espresso powder
1 tbsp sugar (optional, to taste)
2 cups heavy cream
7 oz (200 ml) condensed milk
1 tbsp vanilla extract
Ice cream cones
Garnish with cherries and chocolate flakes

HOW TO MAKE:

On low heat, whisk the sugar, milk, espresso powder and cream in a saucepan until the sugar has dissolved. Add the vanilla extract, stir, and let the mixture chill for a few hours. Add the mix into an ice cream maker, and churn it until you get a thick and smooth mixture. Let it chill in the freezer for a few hours. Scoop the ice cream into wafer cones (optional), and garnish each cone with chocolate flakes and a cherry.

OREO FRAPPE

INGREDIENTS:

Yield: 1

1-2 shots (30-60 ml) of espresso
6 oz (175 ml) milk or coconut milk
2-3 Oreo cookies
Ice cubes
Whipped cream
Garnish with Oreo cookies

HOW TO MAKE:

In a blender half filled with ice, add 1-2 espresso shots, milk, and four Oreo cookies. Blend until smooth. Pour the mixture into a large glass, and top off with whipped cream. Garnish with Oreo cookies.

WHITE RUSSIAN PUDDING

INGREDIENTS:

Yield: 5

1 box instant chocolate pudding (3.9 oz)
14.2 oz (420 ml) milk, chilled and divided
4 oz (120 ml) coffee flavored liqueur, chilled
1 box instant vanilla pudding (3.9 oz)
2 oz (60 ml) vodka, chilled
1 tablespoon instant coffee powder
Whipped cream

HOW TO MAKE:

Make the chocolate coffee liqueur layer by mixing together the chocolate pudding mix, milk, and coffee liqueur. Stir well, and set aside. Make the vodka cream layer by mixing together the vanilla pudding mix, vodka, and milk. Stir well until thickened. Fill a small glass half full with a layer of chocolate coffee liqueur, and then fill the rest with a layer of vanilla vodka. Top off with whipped cream, and garnish with a sprinkle of coffee powder.

COFFEE & BANANA SMOOTHIE

Yield: 1

INGREDIENTS:

1 tbsp of instant coffee powder
4 oz (165 ml) milk (dairy or non-dairy)
6 oz greek yogurt (plain or vanilla)
1 banana (cut into pieces)
1 tbsp of peanut butter
1 tbsp of granulated sugar
Maple syrup (to taste)
1/2 cup ice cubes
Garnish with banana slices

HOW TO MAKE:

In a blender, mix all ingredients for 2-3 minutes until the ice has broken up. Pour the mixture into a large milkshake glass. Garnish with 3-4 banana slices.

ESPRESSO CHOCO MOUSSE

INGREDIENTS:

Yield: 4

3 tbsp espresso powder
3 tbsp brewed coffee
4 oz of dark chocolate
1 cup whipping cream
1 tsp vanilla extract
3 tbsp fine sugar (optional, to taste)
Whipped cream
Garnish with a cherry
and chocolate shavings

HOW TO MAKE:

Combine the espresso, coffee, and cream in a saucepan, and heat the mixture until it almost simmers. Add the chocolate, vanilla extract, and sugar; stir until the chocolate and the sugar are fully dissolved. Pour the mixture into a cocktail glass, and let it chill for a few hours. Garnish the glass with whipped cream, chocolate shavings, and/or a cherry.

COFFEE TIRAMISU

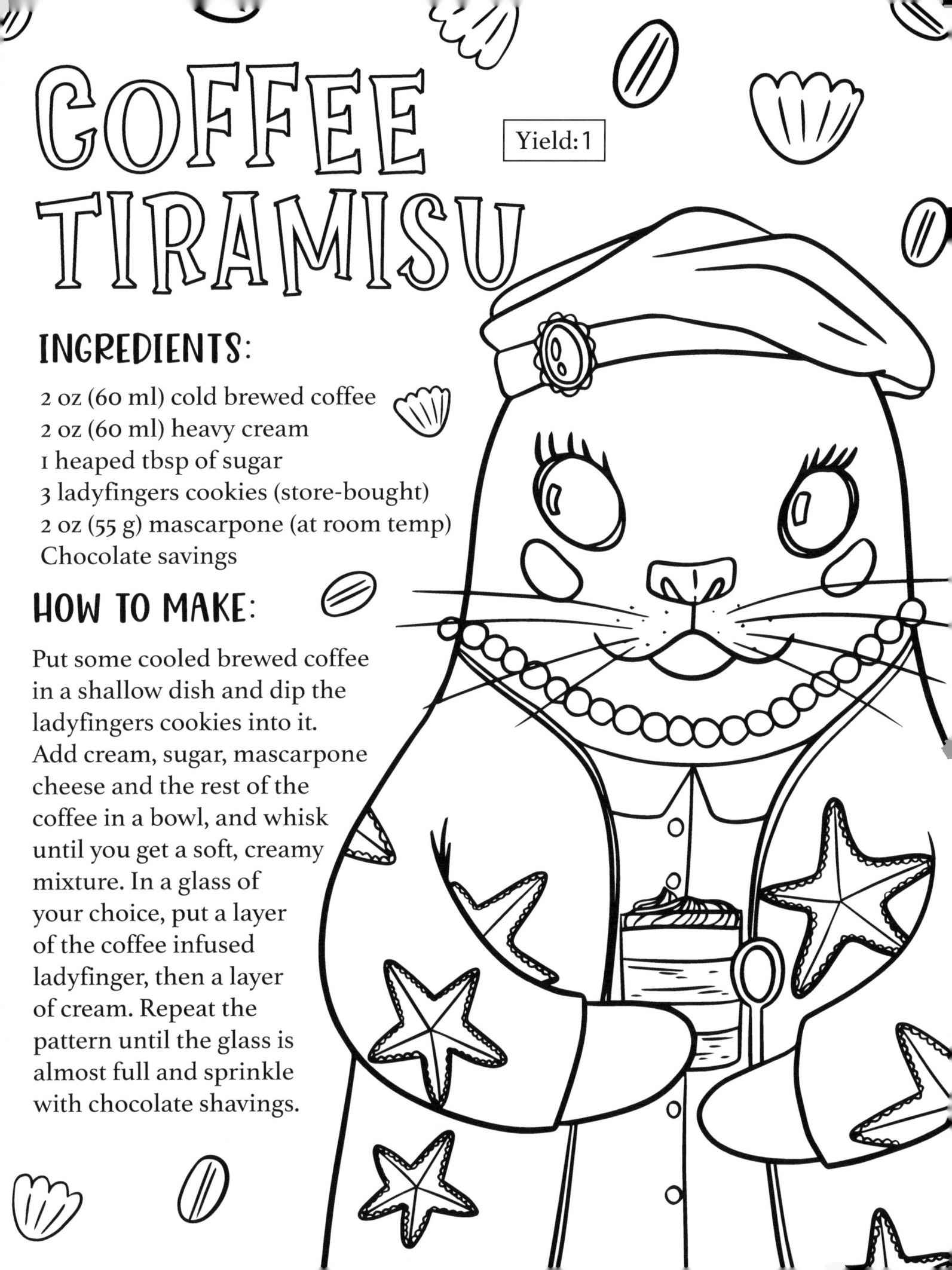

Yield: 1

INGREDIENTS:

2 oz (60 ml) cold brewed coffee
2 oz (60 ml) heavy cream
1 heaped tbsp of sugar
3 ladyfingers cookies (store-bought)
2 oz (55 g) mascarpone (at room temp)
Chocolate savings

HOW TO MAKE:

Put some cooled brewed coffee in a shallow dish and dip the ladyfingers cookies into it. Add cream, sugar, mascarpone cheese and the rest of the coffee in a bowl, and whisk until you get a soft, creamy mixture. In a glass of your choice, put a layer of the coffee infused ladyfinger, then a layer of cream. Repeat the pattern until the glass is almost full and sprinkle with chocolate shavings.

CAFÉ DE OLLA

Yield: 1

INGREDIENTS:

8 oz (235 ml) water
1.5 tbsp dark roast ground coffee
0.5 oz Piloncillo
or 1 tbsp brown sugar
3 cinnamon sticks
1/2 clove
Star anise (optional)

HOW TO MAKE:

In a pan, add water, Piloncillo (or brown sugar), cinnamon sticks, clove and a star anise pod. Bring to a medium heat, and stir until the sugar is completely dissolved and the water comes to a boil. Remove the pan from the heat. Add the ground coffee, and let it steep for 5 minutes. Fine strain the mixture into a mug, and garnish with a cinnamon stick.

COFFEE PANA COTTA

Yield: 6

INGREDIENTS:

12 oz (355 ml) milk
1 tbsp gelatine powder
1 tbsp espresso powder
5 tbsp caster sugar
12 oz (355 ml) cream
1 tbsp vanilla extract
Chocolate sauce
Garnish with chocolate flakes

HOW TO MAKE:

Combine the gelatine powder with the milk over low heat until the powder granules are completely dissolved. Add sugar and stir until the sugar is melted. Next, add the espresso powder, cream and vanilla extract. Stir well until the mixture just comes together. Pour the mixture into serving glasses, add some chocolate sauce an garnish with chocolate flakes.

COFFEE PANCAKES

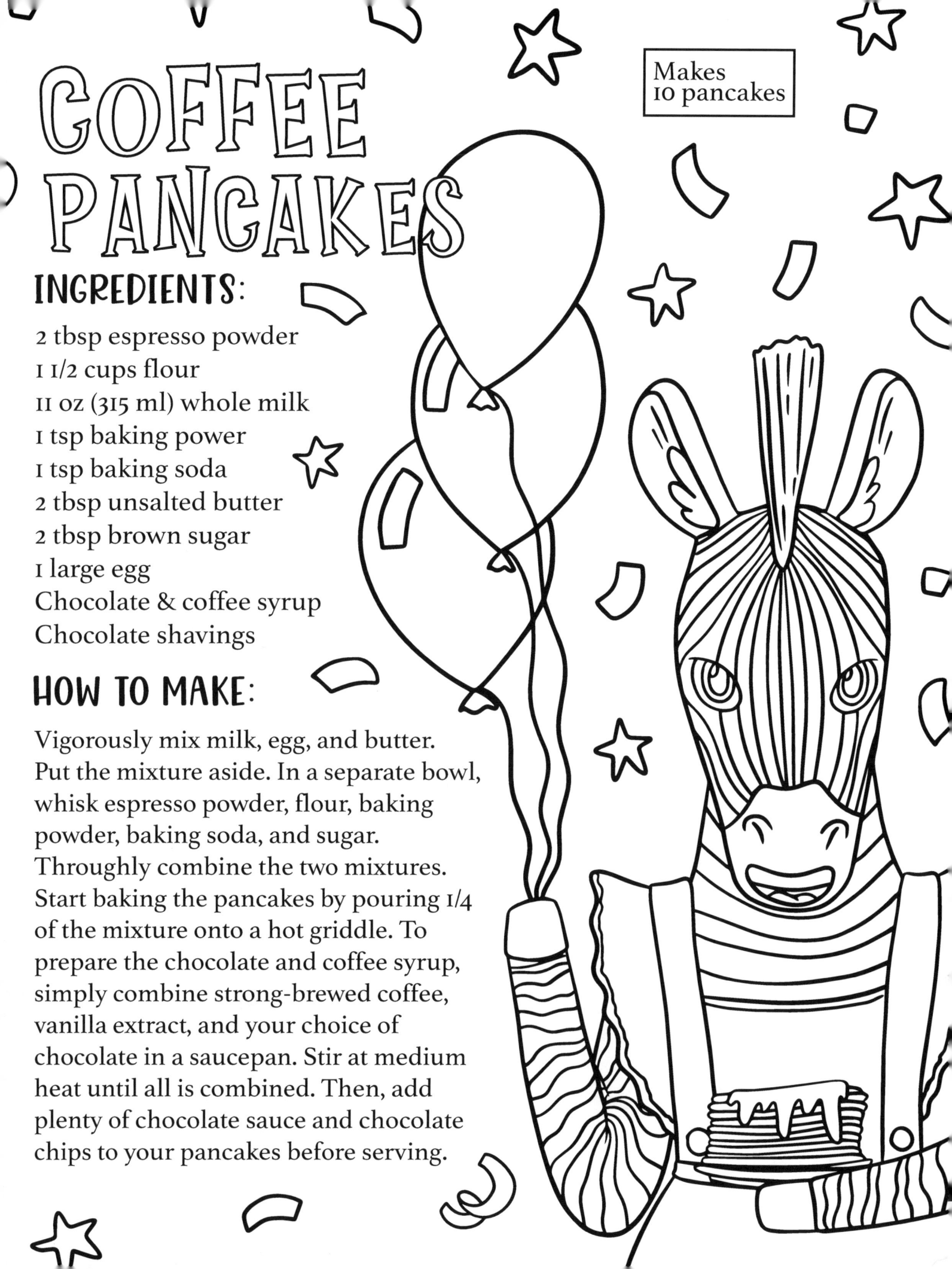

Makes 10 pancakes

INGREDIENTS:

2 tbsp espresso powder
1 1/2 cups flour
11 oz (315 ml) whole milk
1 tsp baking power
1 tsp baking soda
2 tbsp unsalted butter
2 tbsp brown sugar
1 large egg
Chocolate & coffee syrup
Chocolate shavings

HOW TO MAKE:

Vigorously mix milk, egg, and butter. Put the mixture aside. In a separate bowl, whisk espresso powder, flour, baking powder, baking soda, and sugar. Throughly combine the two mixtures. Start baking the pancakes by pouring 1/4 of the mixture onto a hot griddle. To prepare the chocolate and coffee syrup, simply combine strong-brewed coffee, vanilla extract, and your choice of chocolate in a saucepan. Stir at medium heat until all is combined. Then, add plenty of chocolate sauce and chocolate chips to your pancakes before serving.

DALGONA COFFEE

Yield: 1

INGREDIENTS:

2 tbsp instant coffee powder
2 tbsp brown sugar
2 tbsp hot water
Splash of vanilla syrup (optional)
Ice cubes
Milk (diary or non-diary)
Chocolate sprinkles

HOW TO MAKE:

In a bowl, add the instant coffee, hot water, sugar, and a splash of vanilla syrup. Whisk until the sugar is dissolved and the mixture becomes thick. Fill a glass half way with ice cubes. Pour in your choice of milk, leaving a couple of inches at the top of the glass to add your whipped coffee.
Finally, top off your drink with whipped coffee, and garnish with chocolate shavings.

COFFEE JELLY DESERT

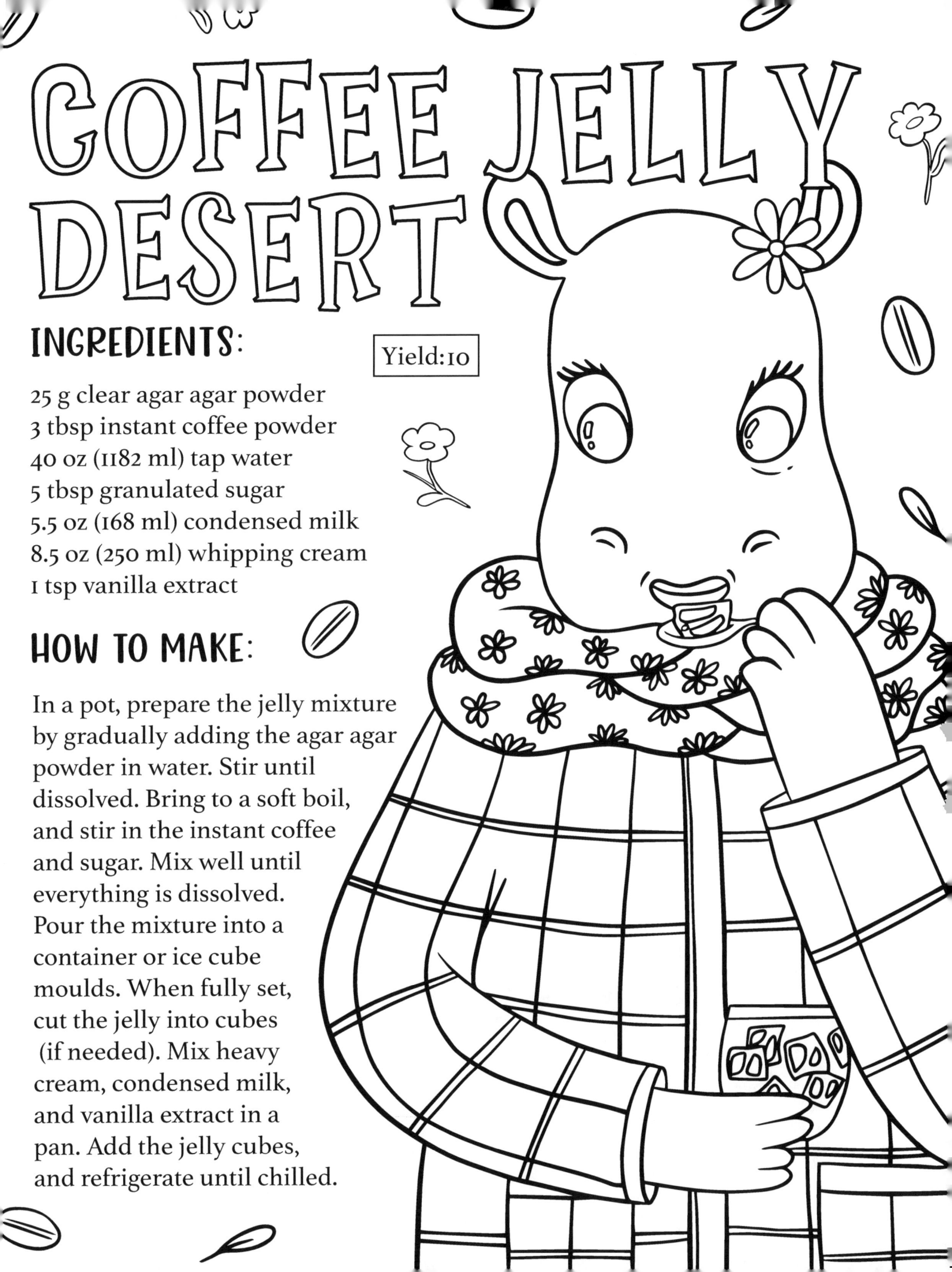

INGREDIENTS:

Yield: 10

25 g clear agar agar powder
3 tbsp instant coffee powder
40 oz (1182 ml) tap water
5 tbsp granulated sugar
5.5 oz (168 ml) condensed milk
8.5 oz (250 ml) whipping cream
1 tsp vanilla extract

HOW TO MAKE:

In a pot, prepare the jelly mixture by gradually adding the agar agar powder in water. Stir until dissolved. Bring to a soft boil, and stir in the instant coffee and sugar. Mix well until everything is dissolved. Pour the mixture into a container or ice cube moulds. When fully set, cut the jelly into cubes (if needed). Mix heavy cream, condensed milk, and vanilla extract in a pan. Add the jelly cubes, and refrigerate until chilled.

LATTE MACCHIATO

Yield: 1

INGREDIENTS:

45 ml brewed coffee
<u>or</u> 1 shot (30 ml) espresso
4 oz (120 ml) frothed milk
1 tsp vanilla extract (optional)
Dash of cocoa powder

HOW TO MAKE:

Prepare an espresso shot or freshly brewed coffee. Heat milk in a pan, and add vanilla extract. Pour the milk in a glass, and whisk it with a mini milk frother until the milk gets foamy. Next, add the espresso shot or the brewed coffee, and sprinkle your latte macchiato with cocoa powder.
All done!

Made in the USA
Columbia, SC
29 November 2023